Why Me?

A Study Guide

Sheilah Steven

PARISH EDUCATION PUBLICATIONS
EDINBURGH

First published in Great Britain
in 1999 by Parish Education Publications
Annie Small House
18 Inverleith Terrace
Edinburgh EH3 5NS

ISBN 0-86153-277-5

Cover design by James Smith
All photographs courtesy of Pathway Productions

Printed and bound in the UK by Hill & Hay Ltd

CONTENTS

ACKNOWLEDGEMENTS

An Oblation by David Adam (*Border Lands*, SPCK, 1991) on page 32-33 is reproduced by kind permission of the publisher.

Many thanks are due to those who participated in the making of the video *Why Me?* Without their willingness to share honestly and openly what the eldership means to them, this whole project would have been the poorer.

To Mure Memorial Parish Church Baillieston, Glasgow: Rev Allan Vint and Anne Carmichael and those now elders, Robert Colquhoun, Peggy McLellan, Aileen and Derek Miller, Carol Rogers and Elizabeth Russell, and the Kirk Session who allowed the camera to invade their training session and ordination service for the making of the video.

To Broughton, Glenholm and Kilbucho linked with Skirling linked with Stobo and Drumelzier linked with Tweedsmuir: Rev Rachel Dobie, John Burnett, Andrew Fox, Sarah Kerr, Elizabeth Reive (for cheerfully persisting with a very wet elder's visit!) and Donald Strathairn, who gave an honest appraisal of the work of the rural elder. To Brian Bushell who allowed us to film in his home.

To St Margaret's Restalrig, Edinburgh: Rev Ewan Aitken, Alistair Cockburn and Kenny McKenzie who gave us an insight into what being an elder means in an Urban Priority Area. To Alison Finlayson for her elder's visit and to Kathy Morrison for allowing us to film in her home.

To Lyndsay Wood of the Kirk of the Holy Rood in Grangemouth who gave us a younger person's perspective.

To the Very Reverend Sandy McDonald who, with a smile, managed, in a few minutes, to explain the tradition and present practice of the Presbyterian system and the place of elders in it.

To Rev Peter Neilson for the narrative.

To all the staff at Pathway Productions who worked above and beyond the call of duty to ensure that we had the best possible video.

Many thanks are also due to those who read the draft text of this booklet and gave constructive criticism:

Rev Dr Frank Bardgett, Secretary Depute, Board of National Mission

Rev Graeme Brown, Elder Trainer in the Presbytery of Orkney

Rev Dr Donald Macaskill, Board of Parish Education

Rev A. Gordon McGillivray, formerly Clerk to the Presbytery of Edinburgh and Assembly Clerk

Mr Ron Lavalette, Elder Trainer in the Presbytery of Ardrossan

Rev Mike Marsden, Training Officer in the United Free Church of Scotland

Mr John Mason, former Elder Trainer in the Presbytery of Inverness

Rev Peter Neilson, Associate Minister at the Parish Church of St Cuthbert

Rev Dr Adrian Varwell, Director of Training at St Ninian's in Crieff

Miss Eileen Walker, Elder Trainer in the Presbytery of Edinburgh

...Paul and Barnabas appointed elders for them in each church and, with prayer and fasting, committed them to the Lord, in whom they had put their trust.

Acts 14 verse 23: New International Version

"Why me?" is the response given by many people when they are asked to consider becoming an elder.

It is worth remembering that the congregation and Kirk Session have already recognised gifts in those approached to be elders. The gifts needed in elders to help Kirk Sessions and congregations to work effectively are many and varied. Here are some suggestions:

- ♫ Faith
- ♫ Listening
- ♫ Valuing others
- ♫ Vision
- ♫ Serving
- ♫ Sharing faith
- ♫ Administration
- ♫ Encouragement
- ♫ Prayer
- ♫ Management
- ♫ Practical skills
- ♫ Openness and honesty
- ♫ Getting alongside others
- ♫ Communication
- ♫ Dependability
- ♫ Commitment
- ♫ Being a team member

Being part of a team is one major element in being an elder. No one person has all the gifts needed to lead the local congregation!

Essentially the call to eldership is a call of God to ministry in his church. This call comes through others: then, generally through discussion with others, reading, prayer and a sense of the inner feeling of the rightness of undertaking the task, God confirms the calling.

It is unlikely that any serving elder feels wholly adequate for the task. What many have learned from experience is that God's grace is sufficient for all He asks of them.

The ability to love God, others and ourselves;

the ability to learn from God, others and ourselves;

the ability to listen to God, others and ourselves;

these abilities increase as the challenges of the eldership are honestly faced.

When Jesus called the disciples into his leadership team, he chose an interesting group. James and John, nicknamed the Sons of Thunder, were called to preach the Gospel of peace and reconciliation (Mark ch. 3 v. 17). Matthew, as a tax collector, was an outsider and probably not the most popular of people (Matthew ch. 9 v. 9-11). Simon Peter found it a bit of a problem understanding what Jesus was really saying (Mark ch. 8 v. 31-33). Thomas needed to be totally convinced and did not trust the word of his friends (John ch. 20 v. 24-25). Simon the Zealot was a freedom fighter with all the attitudes that might entail (Luke ch. 6 v. 15). Yet with these men Jesus turned the world upside down. It is recorded that Mary Magdalene, who had made mistakes in her life, had the privilege of being the first person to see Jesus after the resurrection and was entrusted with telling the others. (Luke ch. 8 v. 2, John ch. 20 v .14-18).

What do elders Promise?

At their service of ordination:

The Minister says:...

> Do you believe the fundamental doctrines of the Christian faith;
> do you promise to seek the unity and peace of this Church;
> to uphold its doctrine, worship, government and discipline;
> and to take your due part in the administration of its affairs?

The elder-elect says:

> **"I do"**

The Minister says:

> "The Lord bless you
> And enable you faithfully to keep this promise."
>
> *Book of Common Order of the Church of Scotland*, p. 337-8

What is meant by the *fundamental doctrines of the Christian Faith*?

The fundamental doctrines are the understanding of God that comes from the Bible.

The Church of Scotland, along with other Presbyterian Churches, "acknowledges the Word of God, contained in the Scriptures of the Old and New Testaments, to be the supreme rule of faith and life. It holds as its subordinate standard the Westminster Confession of Faith." (*Book of Common Order of the Church of Scotland*, p. 337).

The fundamental doctrines may be expressed in the understanding of God shared by the Church through history.

Sometimes a written creed can be found helpful in summarising the essentials of Christian belief. For some, the *Apostles' Creed* is helpful:

> I believe in God, the Father almighty,
> creator of heaven and earth.
> I believe in Jesus Christ,
> God's only Son, our Lord,
> who was conceived by the Holy Spirit,
> born of the Virgin Mary,
> suffered under Pontius Pilate,
> was crucified, died, and was buried;
> he descended to the dead.
> On the third day he rose again;
> he ascended into heaven,
> he is seated at the right hand of the Father,
> and he will come to judge
> the living and the dead.

> I believe in the Holy Spirit,
> the holy catholic Church,
> the communion of saints,
> the forgiveness of sins,
> the resurrection of the body,
> And the life everlasting. Amen.
>
> *Book of Common Order of the Church of Scotland 1996*, p. 16

Some prefer the *Nicene Creed*, also printed in the *Book of Common Order* and in *The Church Hymnary*, Third Edition, number 558.

The fundamental doctrines may be expressed in more contemporary language.

For others, the statement of faith authorised by the General Assembly in 1992 might prove a more useful summary of the fundamental doctrines of the Christian Faith.

We believe in one God:
> Father, Son and Holy Spirit.
> God is love.

We praise God the Father:
> Who created the universe and keeps it in being
> He has made us his sons and daughters to share his joy,
> Living together in justice and peace,
> Caring for his world and for each other.

We proclaim Jesus Christ, God the Son:
> Born of Mary, by the power of the Holy Spirit,
> He became one of us, sharing our life and our death.
> He made known God's compassion and mercy,
> > Giving hope and declaring forgiveness of sin,
> > Offering healing and wholeness to all
> By his death on the cross and by his resurrection
> > He has triumphed over evil.
> > Jesus is Lord of life and of all creation.

We trust God the Holy Spirit:
> Who unites us to Christ and gives life to the Church;
> Who brings us to repentance and assures us of forgiveness.
> The Spirit guides us in our understanding of the bible,
> Renews us in the sacraments,
> And calls us to serve God in the world.

We rejoice in the gift of eternal life:
> We have sure and certain hope of resurrection through Christ,
> And we look for his coming again to judge the world.
> Then all things will be made new;
> And creation will rejoice in worshipping the Father,
> > through the Son, in the power of the Spirit,
> > one God, blessèd for ever.   AMEN

The Church of Scotland Reports to General Assembly (Blue Book) 1992, p. 190

The fundamental doctrines are the understanding of God which is affirmed personally in the vows of membership.

For many, the commitment to eldership seems like an extension of their membership vows. Below are three forms of the membership vows that the General Assembly of the Church of Scotland has authorised.

1935

1. Do you confess your faith in God as your Heavenly Father, in Jesus Christ as your Saviour and Lord and in the Holy Spirit as your Sanctifier?
2. Do you promise, in dependence on Divine Grace, to serve the Lord and to walk in His ways all the days of your life?
3. Do you promise to make diligent use of the means of grace, to share dutifully in the worship and service of the Church, and to give of your substance as the Lord may prosper you, for the advancement of His Kingdom throughout the world?
   I do

Cox, *Practice and Procedure in the Church of Scotland*, p.783

1968

1. Do you believe in one God, Father, Son and Holy Spirit; and do you confess Jesus Christ as your Saviour and Lord?
2. Do you promise to join regularly with your fellow Christians in worship on the Lord's Day?
3. Do you promise to be faithful in reading the Bible, and in prayer?
4. Do you promise to give a fitting proportion of your time, talents and money for the Church's work in the World?
5. Do you promise, depending on the grace of God, to confess Christ before men, to serve Him in your daily work, and to walk in His ways all the days of your life?
   I do

Cox, *Practice and Procedure in the Church of Scotland*, p.783

1996

You have professed with us your faith in one God, Father, Son, and Holy Spirit.

In your baptism God brought you into the household of faith, and in goodness and mercy has shepherded you to this day.

We ask you now to pledge yourself to a life of Christian discipleship:

Do you promise to follow Jesus Christ in your daily life?

**With God's help
I will seek to follow Christ,
and in listening for God's Word,
in the breaking of bread, and prayer,
to grow ever closer to him as the years pass.**

Do you promise to be a faithful member of the Christian community?

**With God's help
I will share in the worship and service of the church,
and in this I will give generously
of what I am and what I have.**

Do you promise to take your part in God's mission to the world?

**With God's help
I will witness to Christ
wherever I find myself
and putting my trust and hope in him
I will seek justice and peace
and the renewing of all life according to God's
promise.**

*Reports to the General Assembly of the Church of Scotland
(Blue Book)* 1996, p. 25/23-4

Only by God's grace can we live out our beliefs. For many, accepting the call to eldership is one more way of putting their beliefs into practice.

Perhaps as prospective elders recognise their God-given gifts and Christ's power to increase them; as they face up to their inadequacies and believe in Christ's power to transform them, the question becomes...

"So why not me?"

For you to consider:

1. Are there any other gifts that you would add to the list at the beginning of this chapter? It might help to think of some elders you know.
2. Are you willing to commit yourself to working alongside those who are already elders in your congregation?
3. Re-read the promise elders make at their ordination. Obtain a copy of the ordination vows for your denomination, if you are being asked to consider eldership other than in the Church of Scotland. If any part is unclear, to whom will you go for clarification?
4. Which of the membership vows is familiar to you? What challenges you most as you read them?
5. What do you think are the strengths and weaknesses you might bring to the eldership? Who would give you some honest feedback on this?

If you are working in a group using the video *Why Me?*...

✤ Watch the complete video.

✤ Discuss:

   1. What did I find most reassuring in the video?

   2. What did I find most challenging?

✤ View sections 1 and 2 (numbering in top left hand corner of the screen).

✤ Discuss:

   1. Are there any other gifts that you would add to the list at the beginning of this chapter?

   2. Read Romans ch.12 v 3-8. Does this say anything to you about eldership?

✤ Read the promise made by elders at their ordination. Obtain a copy of the ordination vows for your denomination if you are being asked to consider eldership other than in the Church of Scotland.

✤ Discuss:

   1. What does this mean to me?

   2. Is anything unclear?

   3. How helpful do you find the statements of faith?

   4. What challenges you most as you read the membership vows?

✤ View sections 4 and 7.

✤ Discuss:

1. *What impresses you about the way the elders on the video responded to the challenge of the eldership?*
2. *What resources have you found helpful in responding to challenges in your own life?*

✤ A prayer from the ordination service for elders:

> Grant [these elders] the gift of your Holy Spirit
> that their hearts may be set on fire
> with love for you
> and for those committed to their care.
> Make them pure in heart
> as those who have the mind of Christ.
> Give them vision to discern your purpose
> for the Church and for the world you love.
> Keep them faithful to the end in all their
> service,
> that, when the chief shepherd appears,
> they may receive glory,
> a crown that never fades.
>
> Blessed be God for all his goodness
> and blessed be his Son Jesus Christ
> and blessed be his Holy Spirit,
> endowing the Church with the fullness of grace
> and making her words the word of life,
> her bread the bread of heaven,
> her shepherding of the flock of God
> his own shepherd work.
>
> And to you, Father, Son and Holy Spirit,
> be glory for ever.
> Amen

(*Book of Common Order of the Church of Scotland*, 1996: p. 338-9)

Where there is no vision, the people perish.
    Proverbs ch. 29 v. 18: Authorised King James Version

Where does the idea originate of the eldership being a visionary, corporate leadership team, enabling the people of God? One of the first mentions of elders being spiritual leaders occurs in the Old Testament.

> The Lord said to Moses: "Bring me seventy of Israel's elders who are known to you as leaders and officials among the people. Make them come to the Tent of Meeting, that they may stand there with you. I will come down and speak with you there, and I will take of the Spirit that is on you and put the Spirit on them. They will help you carry the burden of the people so that you will not have to carry it alone."
> Numbers ch. 11 v. 16 –17, New International Version

Elders are referred to as religious leaders in the days of Jesus. Paul appointed elders in the churches he established. Elders are also mentioned in the book of Revelation as being members of the courts of heaven! It is unclear from the New Testament what the exact role of the elder was, but it was a shared ministry of visionary leadership exercised in each local church.

At the time of the Reformation, John Calvin restored the office of elder in his system of church government. Partly this was to counteract the dominance of the clergy. It also emphasised the ministry of the whole people of God or, as it is sometimes expressed, *the priesthood of all believers.* John Knox brought this system to Scotland and:

> In 1560, the Scottish Parliament officially adopted Protestantism as the nation's religion... The country was divided into parishes. In each parish a Kirk Session was formed consisting of the minister and a number of elders, and once a year the Church would meet in General Assembly to oversee all its work.
> A Gordon McGillivray: *The Church of Scotland,* p. 2

Initially elders were elected to serve for one year but by 1578 in Andrew Melville's *Second Book of Discipline*, elders were to be ordained for life and this remains the present position.

> A new elder is ordained to office, and admitted to the Kirk Session. An elder who leaves a congregation ceases to be a member of its Kirk Session but retains ordained status, and, on becoming a member of another congregation.... If invited to become a member of its Kirk Session, such an elder is admitted, but not re-ordained.
> Ordination and admission both take place at a service of public worship.
>
> *The Constitution and Laws of the Church of Scotland:*
> Ed James L Weatherhead, p.105

How does this idea of the eldership being the visionary, corporate leadership of the local congregation work nowadays?

What are the basic duties of the Kirk Session?

The basic duties of the Kirk Session can be described in the following terms:

1. To be concerned for the spiritual welfare of both the congregation and the parish
2. To regulate the hours of public worship
3. To appoint Communion Sundays
4. To see that all children of members in full communion are baptised
5. To keep records, e.g. Session Minutes, Communion Roll
6. To admit new members
7. To supervise all congregational activities and to ensure that the *Code of Good Practice for the Protection of Children and Young People in the Church* is implemented
8. To encourage members of the congregation in the duties and responsibilities of church membership

9. To commend the gospel to those outwith the Church
10. To attend to instructions and recommendations from the Presbytery and General Assembly
11. To make appointments, e.g. Organist, Church Officer, Presbytery Elder

Most of these duties will be attended to through the regular Kirk Session meeting. How often the Kirk Session meets varies from congregation to congregation and can be affected by the constitution of the individual congregation. In *Quoad Omnia* congregations, where elders have total responsibility for fabric, finance and spiritual matters, the Kirk Session will perhaps meet monthly. Where there is a *Congregational Board, Deacon's Court* or *Committee of Management* dealing with matters of fabric and finance, meetings of the Kirk Session may be less frequent.

The *Moderator* (chair) of the Kirk Session must be, according to the law of the Church, an ordained minister. The *Session Clerk* is usually an elder who is responsible for Kirk Session records and general administration. The choice of session clerk and the length of the appointment are decided by the Kirk Session.

How is the local congregation represented in Presbytery?

Each year an elder is appointed to *Presbytery*. With the minister, they will represent the local congregation. The Presbytery is made up of ministers, elders and members of the diaconate. The Presbytery Elder will attend Presbytery meetings, usually on a monthly basis, and report back the wider concerns to the Kirk Session. The elder may also be asked to be a member of a Presbytery committee. These deal with matters such as Business, Education, Finance, Mission.

The Presbytery will appoint a *Moderator* annually to chair its meetings and be its official representative. The Presbytery Moderator can be any member of Presbytery. The Presbytery also appoints a *Clerk* who is usually one of its members. The *Presbytery Clerk* is responsible for administration, for advising on legal and procedural matters, and also exercises a pastoral role. Because presbyteries have responsibility for a geographic area, they vary enormously in size. Some have representatives from over a hundred congregations, others less than twelve.

How is the local congregation represented at the General Assembly?

The *General Assembly* is the supreme court of the Church and is made up of ministers, elders and members of the diaconate. It decides on matters of policy, doctrine, church law and discipline, among other things. Each Kirk Session will be asked on a rotational basis to nominate a *Commissioner* to the annual General Assembly of the Church of Scotland, held in Edinburgh in May. The *Moderator* of the General Assembly is elected annually. As well as chairing the General Assembly, the Moderator will represent the Church of Scotland in an official capacity. The Church of Scotland does not, like other denominations, have an official spokesperson; so an opinion expressed by a Moderator on a topic that has not been decided upon by the General Assembly is understood to be a purely personal one. Other officials of the Assembly are the *Principal Clerk* and the *Depute Clerk* who together are responsible for overseeing the preparations for each Assembly, keeping a record of proceedings and advising on church law and procedure. The *Procurator* is a Queen's Counsel appointed to advise the Church in regard to civil law.

The General Assembly is served by *Boards* of the Church of Scotland who mainly have their offices at 121 George Street in Edinburgh. The members of the Boards are ministers, elders, members of the diaconate and other members of the church who are nominated for their specific interests and expertise. The Boards serve the Church in many ways e.g. Social Responsibility, World Mission, National Mission, Parish Education, Ministry, Stewardship and Finance, and are always available to support the work of local congregations through their field workers and publications.

How does the Kirk Session operate at local level?

In Presbyterianism, the Kirk Session is the lowest court but it is vitally important to the effective functioning of the whole system. In their book *Leading God's People*, Stewart Matthew and Kenneth Scott state that:

> It is important to remember that the task of the Kirk Session is to lead the whole people of God in that place . . . it is to allow the congregation to exercise its ministry that the Session's work should be geared.

. ...elders need to be encouraged to understand that their leadership involves taking responsibility and making decisions."

Leading God's People: Matthew and Scott, pp. 39 -40

How does this leadership operate at a local level?

Kirk Sessions vary greatly in size and operate in widely differing communities. Many Kirk Sessions operate a *work-group* system where individual elders will be allocated to an area of work that makes special use of their gifts and talents. Such groups might be, e.g., worship, pastoral care, mission, education, communication, youth work. The group might be asked to work on a remit from Presbytery or General Assembly or to look at some local need and how that could be addressed. Their report and suggested action would then be brought to Kirk Session for discussion and decision.

Almost every elder is asked to take responsibility for a particular group of members in the congregation. Usually the elder will visit the *District*, as the group is normally called, on a regular basis. Some elders do not have this responsibility. They may be leaders of a work-group or hold another position of responsibility within the Kirk Session. Their work or family situation might mean that it is unrealistic for them to attempt a district ministry at the present time. A lady elder who requested maternity leave surprised her Kirk Session! Kirk Sessions increasingly offer periods of leave in special circumstances.

How can an elder be an effective member of the Kirk Session?

However the Kirk Session operates, to be an effective member means:

- ✽ Attending Kirk Session meetings as a priority and giving apologies for unavoidable absence to the Session Clerk

- ✽ Reading the agenda and any other papers well before the meeting

- ✽ Praying for the Kirk Session, the Moderator and the church family. *Pray Now* published annually by the Panel of Worship, is found by many to be helpful for this.

- ✽ Keeping informed of local and national issues. *Life and Work*, the Church of Scotland monthly magazine, is a very useful publication for understanding current church issues.

᪾ Putting items of concern on the agenda before the meeting. Don't bring them up when everyone is ready to go home!

᪾ Listening carefully to your fellow elders, members and community.

᪾ Asking questions. Perhaps you are not the only one who does not fully understand what is being discussed!

᪾ Saying what you think. Sometimes God's Spirit can be at work when you feel uneasy about something.

᪾ Keeping to the point. Save the interesting anecdote for when it really has something to say to the situation!

᪾ Volunteering to help. The Minister and Session Clerk are not responsible for doing everything!

᪾ Encouraging others to help. There may be others outwith the Kirk Session who might become involved in a project if you asked them to help.

᪾ Remembering you are part of a team and are not expected to do everything and know everything.

᪾ Remembering loyalty to your minister, fellow elders and church family.

᪾ Remembering confidentiality. Session meetings are confidential. You do not decide what is confidential. You are not free to discuss the content with others unless you are permitted to do so.

In Ephesians ch. 4 v. 15- 16, speaking to the church community, Paul says:

> (by) speaking the truth in love, we will in all things grow up into him who is the Head, that is Christ. From him the whole body, joined and held together by every supporting ligament, grows and builds itself up in love, as each part does its work.
>
> New International Version

As the Head of each congregation is Christ, speaking the truth in love becomes essential for those privileged to be called as leaders. Any leader, or member, who is not using their gifts to the full in Christ's service, hinders the effectiveness of the church. The Assembly Council reflects this thought. In their report to the General Assembly of 1990 they said:

Kirk Sessions could find it helpful to consider ...how they could, from the resources already within the congregation, create a more meaningful team approach to ministry and mission in their parish.

Reports to the General Assembly (Blue Book), 1990, p.93

The call to leadership as an elder is a challenge as well as a privilege. Leading by example can be a demanding role. It is certainly not a commitment to be taken lightly.

Rev Peter Neilson, the former Director of Training at St Ninian's in Crieff, has summed up this challenge in the following way:

The church of today and tomorrow is a church in transition in the midst of a society in the midst of change. The role of the Kirk Session today must be more dynamic, steering a wise course through uncharted waters.

The need is not only for careful administration but for adventurous, caring and courageous leadership.

For you to consider:

1. Find out the time commitment involved in being a member of your Kirk Session.
   - ✤ How often does the Session meet?
   - ✤ Will you be expected to join a Session workgroup?
   - ✤ How many Sundays in the year will you be on duty? What will that duty entail?
   - ✤ Will you automatically become a member of the Congregational Board?
   - ✤ Will you have an elder's district? How many homes will you be expected to visit and how often?
2. Does your congregation have a mission or a vision statement?
3. Leadership by example is a concern to many elders. What are your concerns in this area? With whom might you discuss them? See 1 Timothy ch. 3 v. 8-13.
4. Praying for the Church, both locally and nationally, can be a challenge for elders. *Pray Now*, the daily devotional guide published annually in March for the Panel on Worship by Saint Andrew Press, contains original prayers, material for reflection and specific intercessions for the work and personnel of the Church of Scotland. Might this publication be of help to you?
5. *Life and Work*, the monthly magazine of the Church of Scotland, offers a wide variety of interesting material to help elders keep informed. Might this be a useful resource for you?
6. What does the historic nature of the role of eldership mean for you? Further information on this aspect can be found in: pp. 7-19 in *Leading God's People*: Matthew & Scott; pp. 655-659 in 'Appendix to the Report of the Panel on Doctrine', *Reports to the General Assembly* (*the Blue Book*), 1967; pp. 1-7, *The Church of Scotland*: A. Gordon McGillivray
7. What advantages and disadvantages do you think the Presbyterian form of church government has?
   Further information on this can be found in: pp. 8 & 13-22, *The Church of Scotland*: A. Gordon McGillivray.
   Further reference works:
   The Law and Practice of the Kirk: Andrew Herron.
   The Constitution and Laws of the Church of Scotland (the Green Book): ed. James L. Weatherhead.

If you are working in a group using the video "Why Me?"...

✤ Watch section 3 of the video.

✤ Sandy McDonald, a former Moderator of the General Assembly of the Church of Scotland, says, 'Women and men who are elders are key people in terms of the working of the Presbyterian Church.'

✤ Discuss *to what extent you think this is true.*

✤ Elizabeth Russell, now an elder in Mure Memorial Church, says 'You need vision. You need to be open to what is out there and what can be done in the community and the parish.' Discuss the vision you have for your congregation and parish.

✤ Watch section 5 of the video.

✤ St Margaret's Church, Restalrig have the following statement of intent:

> We strive to be an open, lively, positive-thinking congregation. We are rooted in the Church of Scotland tradition but work and worship with congregations of all denominations. We are concerned for the problems of our world, such as homelessness, racism, violence against women, poverty, hunger or discrimination of any type. We try to meet some of those needs in our community through the work of the Ripple Project* and other activities. We support international organisations such as Christian Aid and Traidcraft, who work to meet those needs in other places. We strive to be an equal opportunities employer and to ensure our facilities and activities are accessible for everyone.

* The Ripple project is a church/community initiative which provides free community information and assistance, an older person's social club, a lunch club, a parent/carer toddler group, an after-school club, a confidential listening service, a youth volunteer scheme and a referral group to help young people with behavioural difficulties.

✥ Discuss:

> *how useful a statement of intent like this might be for the visionary leadership of a congregation.*

✥ Ewan Aitken, minister of St Margaret's says that in his Kirk Session,

> 'We have a five year plan with three main goals. Each of the nine committees has targets.'

✥ Discuss:

> *whether this kind of structure is at work in the Kirk Session leadership of your congregation.*

✥ Listening to the elders and Minister of Mure Memorial in Baillieston, Glasgow, how would you sum up their leadership vision for their parish?

✥ Listening to the elders and Minister of Upper Tweed-dale (you may need to view section 4 again) how would you sum up their leadership vision for their parishes?

. . . Fellow elders, this is my plea to you: feed the flock of God; care for it willingly, not grudgingly; not for what you will get out of it, but because you are eager to serve the Lord.

1 Peter ch. 5 v. 1- 2: The Living Bible Paraphrased

Caring for others has been a traditional part of an elder's role. In both the Old and New Testaments this aspect is highlighted, as can be seen from the above quotation and the way in which the elders from Moses' time were urged to help carry the burden of the people (cf. p. 15). In Andrew Melville's *Second Book of Discipline* (1578), it is stated that:

The office of elder includes the visitation of the sick, of prisoners and of the poor, catechising in the homes, assisting at the Sacraments and reading the Scriptures and Prayers in the absence of a Minister.

Partnership

In today's church, caring for the parish is seen as a partnership between the minister and the elder. For some elders their pastoral role may be caring for the members of the youth club. For others it might be caring for a group of older people in the parish. For still others it might be working with a group of those enquiring about the faith. However, for the majority of elders their pastoral role will be caring for a number of members and their families, usually in a specific area of the parish. The elder will assume responsibility for visiting people in their homes on a regular basis. Sometimes this will be linked to inviting people to Communion services. At other times it will be in times of happiness and celebration, or in times of difficulty. Some elders deliver a monthly magazine which increases their contact with their *District*, as the group is usually known.

Pastoral Visiting

The First Visit

For a new elder the first visit can be a daunting prospect. Some Kirk Sessions will encourage the previous elder, the session clerk or the minister to accompany the new elder on the first visit. Whether or not an accompanied visit is appropriate, it can be helpful if the previous elder, session clerk or minister tells the new elder something about the families in the district. In this way the new elder is more prepared for the first visit. In other situations, the members might be informed by letter of the appointment of the new elder or the new elder might phone the member to introduce himself or herself and arrange an appropriate time to visit.

Why Visit?

What is the purpose of the visit?

> To each elder ...there is normally assigned a district for the care of which [(s)he] is responsible. [Each elder, in partnership with the Minister, cares for] the sick, the aged and the needy and encourages those outside the fellowship of the church.
>
> *Caring for God's People*: Matthew & Lawson (adapted), citing Pardovan, p. 14

The above quotation gives a reasonable definition of the present day task. It assumes that the elder has built up good relationships and is welcome in the home. For the elder, chatting to people in church, in the take-away queue or at the bowling green are also opportunities to build better relationships. Pastoral care does not only take place on the home visit! Sometimes elders will need to create opportunities to meet informally with members of the District and their families. A district supper, study evening or barbecue might be appropriate. These can all help in the essential task of building good relationships.

Prayer

In some situations where there may be previous hurt, building up a level of trust with people can take a long time and need a lot of patience and prayer. As Rev George Wilkie says, the sure test of the concern of an elder for his/her people will be the urgency with which (s)he prays for them:

> Some will remember one family by name every day, others will try to cover all the families once per week. Methods may vary, but the beginning of any efforts to serve the members of a district in God's name must be knowing them in God's presence.
>
> Quoted in *Caring for God's People*, p. 30

Praying for those visited, fellow elders, the minister and parish can rightly be considered part of the elder's spiritual role. But what about praying with those who are visited? Is this a purpose of the elder's visit?

Few elders pray with everyone they visit. A common response from elders is that they would pray with anyone who asked them. Perhaps the experienced elder who honestly said, 'Thank God no-one has ever asked me', was expressing the thoughts of many! However, some elders will carry a prayer card for this eventuality. Others would be ready to share the Lord's Prayer or to say the words of Psalm 23 as a prayer when they visit. Yet others are prepared to say a short, simple prayer as appropriate. As an elder leaves a home, perhaps saying 'God bless you', is as simple a prayer as any.

Faith Sharing

It is a special privilege for an elder when faith can be openly discussed and shared on a visit. For most elders this happens infrequently. It can be stimulated, for example, by what some notable church leader has said or done; by a discussion on favourite hymns; by a family celebration or crisis. The emphasis is on elders sharing honestly what is meaningful for them, not on having the "right" answer or telling people what to believe. Building up a relationship where this kind of sharing is possible could be considered a further purpose of the elder's visit

Keeping in Touch

Pastoral visiting is also about communication. The elder is a vital link in keeping the minister, the people, the parish and the Kirk Session informed.

Communication does not consist only of information but is about needs, hopes, expectations, faith and love. This aspect is emphasised in the following quotation:

> God cares for each one as a person beloved and precious and unique, not simply as one who has a function to perform in God's plan. Pastoral visiting represents that loving, caring relationship. The pastor visits every member of the congregation, not because they are influential or helpful, but simply because they are God's children to be loved and respected as they are.
>
> Lesslie Newbigin; quoted in *Thank God You've Come*,
> Graham Long, p. 27

The purpose of general visiting could be summed up as

- ♭ building relationships
- ♭ encouraging faith
- ♭ communication

Special Concerns

Elders can have special concerns about visiting in times of difficulty.

> 'Could I helpfully visit someone who had been bereaved?'
> 'Would I be any use visiting someone who was terminally ill?'
> 'What good would I be visiting someone suffering from dementia?'
> 'What would I say to someone who was going through a divorce?'

Elders might be concerned that they have no personal experience of the situation and do not understand the issues involved. The video and discussion pack *Caring for God's People*, available from the Church of

Scotland's Board of Parish Education, has been found by Kirk Sessions to be useful in addressing these natural concerns. Presbytery Elder Trainers can also provide practical training on pastoral visiting, leadership, prayer and faith-sharing.

Listening

It is also worth remembering that when people are experiencing difficult times they often find it valuable to have someone who will listen to them without necessarily offering them advice. One of the essential skills in pastoral visiting is listening. The value of being alongside, of accompanying those going through difficult times, should not be underestimated.

Teamwork

Occasions may arise when elders feel out of their depth. It is at times like these when the team nature of the eldership is relevant. Assistance can be sought from the minister, the session clerk, fellow elders, or others of experience within the congregation. Referring to others is not a sign of weakness but is a sign of real care. Networking is something in which churches can excel as long as confidentiality is respected. Some churches have developed pastoral care teams where elders, pastoral visitors and members with special gifts will work together to care for an area, usually of about 3 to 6 elders' districts joined together. As well as offering more flexibility in the way pastoral care is offered, this system ensures that those providing the care are themselves supported and cared for by the rest of the area team. A fuller explanation of this scheme is given in *Leading God's People*, Matthew & Scott, p. 95; see also p. 125, 'A Care Visiting Scheme' .

However pastoral care is organised, elders need to remember that they do not bear the sole responsibility. Anything that troubles them needs to be shared with the appropriate person. There may be clashes of personality, difficulty in getting over the doorstep or too much work for a hard-pressed elder to do. In spite of the difficulties, the majority of elders find that district visiting is the most satisfying part of an elder's role. They enjoy it! The privilege of walking alongside others has enriched their life and their faith.

For you to consider:

1. What do you see as the challenges facing you in the pastoral role of the elder?
2. Who or what do you see as the main resources for meeting those challenges?
3. Here is an outline prayer that could be used on a pastoral visit.
   > Loving God,
   > We thank you that you are always with us.
   > Bless _____(names of those for whom you are praying) with your peace and strength.
   > In Jesus' name, Amen.

   How comfortable would you feel using a prayer like this?
   Are there any other prayers you might use?
4. Where do you think communication breaks down in your congregation? How might you improve the situation?
5. Do you really believe elders enjoy visiting? Ask some and find out!

If you are working in a group using the video *Why Me?* . . .

✎ Watch section 6
✎ Anne Carmichael, an elder in Mure Memorial says her concerns were,
   > 'How will I help people when they have a bereavement?'
   > 'What if people ask difficult questions that I don't know the answer to?'
✎ Carol Rodgers, now an elder in Mure Memorial says her concerns were,
   > 'How often will I need to visit? How much time will I need to give?'
✎ Discuss: *the answers you would give to these questions.*
✎ Ewan Aitken, minister of St Margaret's, Restalrig says that elders need to ask themselves:
   > 'Not "How do we survive?" But, "How do we grow? How do we develop?"'
✎ Discuss:
   > *how you can enable growth and development in yourself and in those for whom you have a pastoral responsibility.*

30

But Moses said, "O Lord, please send someone else to do it."
The Lord said, "..I will help both you and Aaron speak and will teach you
what to do."

Exodus ch. 4 v. 13-15: New International Version

When asked to take on a special responsibility like eldership, many can sympathise with Moses' reaction. Someone once said that God never calls people to a task without providing them with the resources to accomplish that task. Sometimes it might not feel that way! The Very Rev Sandy McDonald, a former Moderator of the General Assembly, in section 7 of the video *Why Me?*, has said of being an elder that: 'This could be one of the most fulfilling, thrilling and spiritual experiences of your whole life.'

Lyndsay Wood, an elder in her early twenties from the Kirk of the Holy Rood in Grangemouth, has said that in her experience being an elder is: 'Very exciting and very interesting. I'm prepared to take on that commitment.'

Derek Miller, an elder in Mure Memorial Church in Baillieston, Glasgow has said: 'What is life, if you don't have a commitment?'

Once individuals approached to consider eldership have agreed to that nomination, an Edict will be read to the congregation on the two Sundays prior to the date fixed for the ordination service. If members of the congregation have any objections to the life or doctrine of those nominated they have an opportunity to inform the Kirk Session at an appointed time. If there are no objections the service of ordination may proceed.

During the service elders-elect will say "I do" to the eldership promise (see the first chapter) and then *Sign the Formula* as a sign of the acceptance of its terms and of the promise just made. The wording of the Formula is:

> I believe the fundamental doctrines of the Christian Faith contained in the Confession of Faith of this Church.
>
> I acknowledge the Presbyterian government of this Church to be agreeable to the Word of God, and promise that I will submit thereto and concur therewith.
>
> I promise to observe the order of worship and the administration of all public ordinances as the same are or may be allowed in this Church.

James T Cox: *Practice and Procedure in the Church of Scotland*, p. 395

They will then receive the *right hand of fellowship* from some or all of their fellow elders and be welcomed to their new role and responsibility. As in the days of the early Church when people were set apart for a special ministry, they had hands laid on their heads (Acts ch. 13 v. 2-3) so the right hand of fellowship can be seen in a similar way, to recognise the call of God.

Is the call to eldership for you?

As, Donald Strathairn, Session Clerk of Broughton, Glenholm and Kilbucho, has said, 'Ask, ask, ask and pray.'

This prayer by David Adam might be of help as you consider your response:

I place my hands in yours Lord
I place my hands in yours

I place my will in yours Lord
I place my will in yours

I place my days in yours Lord
I place my days in yours

I place my thoughts in yours Lord
I place my thoughts in yours

I place my heart in yours Lord
I place my heart in yours

All that I am I give you Lord
All that I am I give

All that I have I share with you Lord
All that I have I share with you.

All my life is yours Lord
All my life is yours

All my desires are yours Lord
All my desires are yours

All my hopes are in you Lord
All my hopes are in you

All I want is you Lord
All I want is you.

'An Oblation'; *Border Lands*, p. 94-95

The challenge of eldership is a challenge to commitment but God is wholly committed to his people.

Leadership

Books

Leading God's People, Matthew and Scott, St Andrew Press: Edinburgh, 1995

The Church of Scotland, A. Gordon McGillivray, St Andrew Press: Edinburgh, 1996

The Law and Practice of the Kirk, Andrew Herron, Chapter House: Glasgow 1995

The Constitution and Laws of the Church of Scotland, ed James L. Weatherhead, Board of Practice and Procedure: Edinburgh, 1997

Practice and Procedure in the Church of Scotland, James T. Cox, Sixth Edition, ed. D.F.M. Macdonald, Committee on General Administration, the Church of Scotland: Edinburgh 1976 (out of print).

Video

Why Me? with accompanying booklet, Parish Education Publications, Board of Parish Education, 18 Inverleith Terrace, Edinburgh EH3 5NS, 0131 332 0343

Towards Tomorrow, Board of National Mission, 121 George Street, Edinburgh EH2 4YN, 0131 225 5722

Courses (available locally):

Through Presbytery elder Trainers: contact Board of Parish Education: 0131 332 0343.

Exploring eldership

Being an elder

Leading Small Groups

Leading Worship

Courses (available locally) cont.:

Through Mission Advisers, contact National Mission at St Brycedale Church Centre, Kirkcaldy: 01592 646406

Congregational Mission Design
From Contact to Integration

Courses (available residentially):

Exploring Eldership (Board of Parish Education)
(0131 332 0343)
Being an Elder Today parts 1 & 2
Being on a Congregational Board
(St Ninian's Training Centre, Crieff 01764 653766)

Pastoral

Books

Caring for God's People, Matthew & Lawson, Saint Andrew Press: Edinburgh 1995

Video

Caring for God's People, with accompanying booklet, Parish Education Publications, Board of Parish Education: 18 Inverleith Terrace, Edinburgh EH3 5NS: 0131 332 0343

Courses (available locally through Presbytery Elder Trainers):

Learning to Care
The Next Step
Praying with People
Something to Share (also through Mission Advisers)

Courses (available residentially)

Caring for God's People: Board of Parish Education and at St Ninian's Centre in Crieff

Devotional:

Guides:

Pray Now, Panel on Worship, Saint Andrew Press: published annually in
March, also available on tape
Scripture Union Quarterly Bible Reading Notes:
Alive to God & *Closer to God* (amalgamated)
Daily Bread (also in large type)
Encounter with God:
Bible Reading Fellowship (three issues per year):
Guidelines
New Daylight (also in large print)
all from Bible Reading Fellowship, Peter's Way, Sandy Lane West,
Oxford, OX4 5HG: Tel 01865 748227
The Upper Room; bi-monthly from Methodist Publishing House; Every Day
with Jesus

Books:

Eddie Askew: *A Silence and a Shouting*, Leprosy Mission, 1982; *Cross
Purposes*, Leprosy Mission, 1995; *Disguises of Love*, Leprosy Mission,
1983.
David Adam: *Border Lands* (London: SPCK, 1991), *The Edge of Glory*,
London: SPCK, 1985.
Rowland Croucher: *Rivers in the Desert*, Lion: 1991; *Sunrise-Sunset*, Collins
Dove, Australia, 1996
John Baillie: *A Diary of Private Prayer*: O.U.P.; 1994; a classic book of prayers
for the month
J. Philip Newell: *Each Day and Each Night*, Wild Goose Publications, 1994
Ian M. Reid: *Meditations from the Iona Community*, Wild Goose Publications, 1998

Other works referred to:

The Book of Common Order of the Church of Scotland, St Andrew Press,
Edinburgh 1996
Thank God You've Come, Graham Long, U.R.C. House; 1992

The Living Bible Paraphrased, ed. K N Taylor, Kingsway, 1998
The Law and Practice of the Kirk, Andrew Herron, Chapter House Ltd:
Glasgow: 1995